W9-CUK-717

SECRETS OF

HABITATS

ANDREW SOLWAY

Marshall Cavendish
Benchmark
New York

This edition first published in 2011 in the United States of America
by MARSHALL CAVENDISH BENCHMARK
An imprint of Marshall Cavendish Corporation

This publication represents the opinions and views of the author based on Andrew Solway's personal experience, knowledge, and research. The information in this book serves as a general guide only. The author and publisher have used their best efforts in preparing this book and disclaim liability rising directly and indirectly from the use and application of this book.

Planned and produced by Discovery Books Ltd., 2 College Street, Ludlow, Shropshire, SY8 1AN www.discoverybooks.net
Managing editor: Paul Humphrey
Editor: Clare Hibbert
Designer: sprout.uk.com Limited
Illustrators: Peter Bull (page 9), Stefan Chabluk, Stuart Lafford (page 6)
Picture researcher: Tom Humphrey

Photo acknowledgments: Corbis: pp 7 (Seth Resnick/Science Faction), 15 (Christophe Boisvieux), 18 (Tony Waltham/Robert Harding World Imagery), 27 (Steven Kazlowski/Science Faction), 28 (Martin Harvey); FLPA: p 24 (Nigel Cattlin); Getty Images: pp 11 (Zeb Andrews), 12 (Grambo), 14 (Tom Brakefield), 16 (Michael Fogden), 20 (Masaaki Tanaka / Sebun Photo), 25 (Coke Whitworth); IStockphoto: cover desert (gioadventures), cover cactus (jlvphoto), cover tree frog (Snowleopard1), pp 1 and 8 (Edwin van Wier), 17 (Liz Leyden), 22 (Peter Muckherjee), 26 (David Hills); Shutterstock Images: pp 5 (Chris Curtis), 19 (Danny Warren), 21 (Simone van den Berg), 23 (Vaklav).

Other Marshall Cavendish Offices:
Marshall Cavendish International (Asia) Private Limited, 1 New Industrial Road, Singapore 536196 • Marshall Cavendish International (Thailand) Co Ltd. 253 Asoke, 12th Flr, Sukhumvit 21 Road, Klongtoey Nua, Wattana, Bangkok 10110, Thailand • Marshall Cavendish (Malaysia) Sdn Bhd, Times Subang, Lot 46, Subang Hi-Tech Industrial Park, Batu Tiga, 40000 Shah Alam, Selangor Darul Ehsan, Malaysia

Marshall Cavendish is a trademark of Times Publishing Limited

The website addresses (URLs) included in this book were valid at the time of going to press. However, because of the nature of the Internet, it is possible that some addresses may have changed, or the sites may have changed or closed down since publication. While the author, packager, and the publisher regret any inconvenience this may cause to the readers, no responsibility for any such changes can be accepted by the author, packager, or publisher.

Every attempt has been made to clear copyright. Should there be any inadvertent omission, please apply to the publisher for rectification.

Library of Congress Cataloging-in-Publication Data

Solway, Andrew.
  Secrets of habitats / Andrew Solway.
      p. cm. -- (Science secrets)
  Includes bibliographical references and index.
  ISBN 978-1-60870-137-7
  1. Habitat (Ecology)--Juvenile literature. I. Title.
  QH541.14.S67 2011
  577--dc22
                        2010003940

Printed in China
1 3 6 5 4 2

Contents

What Are Habitats?

A habitat is a place where an animal or plant lives. There are many different kinds of habitat. A river is one kind of habitat, while a desert is another kind.

Shaping a Habitat

What a habitat is like depends partly on the climate—the average weather in the area over a long period of time. In a desert it rarely rains, while in rain forests it rains a lot of the time.

The kind of rocks and landscape also affect the habitat, and so do living things. A forest would not be a forest without trees.

The Biggest Habitats

Some habitats cover large areas. Oceans cover two-thirds of the earth's surface, while **conifer** forests cover a little over one-tenth of the land area. These large habitats are known as **biomes**.

▼ *A map of the world's biomes. The largest is the water biome that includes rivers, lakes, and oceans.*

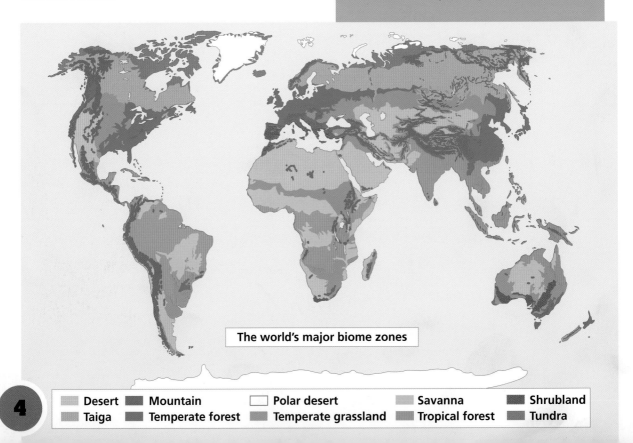

The world's major biome zones

Desert	Mountain	Polar desert	Savanna	Shrubland
Taiga	Temperate forest	Temperate grassland	Tropical forest	Tundra

▲ *Monument Valley in Utah is an example of a desert habitat. It is very dry, with little plant life.*

Each biome can be split into smaller and smaller habitats. For insects, the forest floor is a very different habitat from a leafy treetop.

In this book, you will discover all kinds of habitats, from rotting logs to the wide oceans. You will also learn how human beings affect habitats and the living things in them.

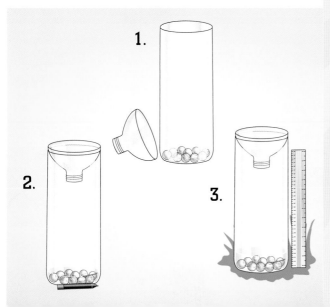

EXPERIMENT

MEASURING RAINFALL

Measure the rainfall in a local habitat for one month. The amount of rainfall affects what the habitat is like.

You will need:
• a small plastic bottle • some marbles • some water • a permanent marker • a ruler • a pen • a notebook

1. Ask an adult to cut the top off the bottle. Put a layer of marbles in the bottom to weight it down.

2. Turn the top upside down and push it into the bottle. This will cut down on water loss through **evaporation**. Add water to just cover the marbles. Mark the water level with the marker.

3. Put the bottle outside in an open area. After a day, use the ruler to measure from the mark to the level of the water. This is the rainfall for that day. Write it down.

4. Pour out the water (but not the marbles), and then fill up the bottle to the mark again. The next day, measure from the mark to the water level again.

5. Repeat for the rest of the month, then add up your figures. How much rain fell?

How Do Habitats Work?

Every living thing needs certain things to survive and grow. Plants need light, carbon dioxide (a gas in the air), water, and minerals (chemicals in the soil). Animals need water, food, and shelter.

Living things also need others of the same **species** (kind), so that they can **breed** and produce **offspring** (babies).

Providing the Essentials

For an **organism** to get all it needs from its habitat, it requires a certain amount of space. Many creatures might share the same space, but most need slightly different things.

The space that an animal needs to find enough food for survival is called its **territory**. Caterpillars may have a territory of just one plant. Other animals need much more space.

Wolverines are weasel-like **predators** of the far north. To catch enough **prey**, each needs a territory of more than 200 square miles (500 square kilometers).

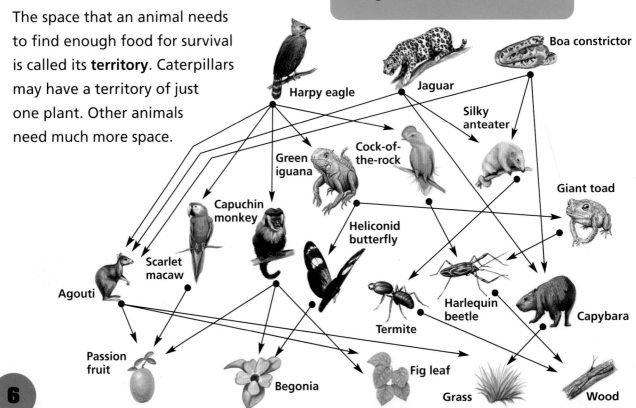

▼ *A food web from the Amazon rain forest. At the bottom are plants, which make their own food. Above them are plant-eating animals, then meat-eaters.*

Harpy eagle

Jaguar

Boa constrictor

Silky anteater

Green iguana

Cock-of-the-rock

Giant toad

Capuchin monkey

Heliconid butterfly

Scarlet macaw

Agouti

Harlequin beetle

Termite

Capybara

Passion fruit

Begonia

Fig leaf

Grass

Wood

► Most mammals are land animals, but seals are adapted to living in the sea. They have thick layers of blubber (fat) to protect them from the cold.

Chains and Webs

The animals and plants in a habitat rely on each other in various ways. One species may depend on another for food. A rabbit needs grass to eat, while a fox needs rabbits and other prey animals to survive. Another species may need help to **reproduce**. Many flowers could not survive without bees to carry their **pollen** from plant to plant.

Organisms also depend on each other for shelter. Many animals live in trees, while fleas, for instance, live in the feathers of birds or the fur of mammals.

SCIENCE SECRETS

MUTUAL BENEFITS

Aphids are small insects that eat only plant **sap**. Some ant species keep "herds" of aphids, much like human farmers keep cattle. The ants feed on a sugary liquid called honeydew that the aphids produce. The aphids benefit too, because the ants protect them from predators.

What Is the Biggest Biome?

Water can be described as one huge biome, but it contains many different habitats. They include the rivers, streams, and lakes that flow into the oceans.

Rivers and lakes are fresh water, while seas are salty. The seas around coral reefs are warm, light-filled, and brimming with life. The ocean depths, however, are cold and dark and little life exists there.

Food Connections

As on land, water creatures are connected through food chains and webs. In the ocean, there are microscopic plantlike creatures called **phytoplankton**. Like land plants, they make their own food from water, carbon dioxide, and light.

Tiny animals called **zooplankton** feed on these microscopic plants. The animal and plant plankton drift with the currents and provide food for larger animals.

▼ *Coral reefs grow in warm, shallow waters. They are the richest habitats in the ocean.*

Freshwater Life

There are far more large plants in rivers, lakes, and ponds than in the sea. Some plants float or grow on the bottom. Others thrive along banks and shores. All these plants provide food for animals that live in or near the water. Insects are common in and around fresh water but not in the ocean.

Damaged Habitats

Many water habitats have been damaged by human activities. Fishing fleets take thousands of tons of fish from seas and oceans each day. Waters have also become polluted by oil spills, **sewage**, and mining wastes.

SPECIAL SHRIMP

There are more species of crustaceans than of any other marine animals. They include crabs, lobsters, and shrimps.

The mantis shrimp is a small seabed predator. It spots prey with its incredible eyes, which can pick up **ultraviolet light**—a kind of light that is invisible to humans. The shrimp shoots out its front legs to snatch prey at lightning speed. It has the fastest-moving limbs on earth!

▼ *A lake has three main zones: the shallow margin or edge, the muddy bottom, and open water. The edge is often hidden by reeds, irises, and other water plants.*

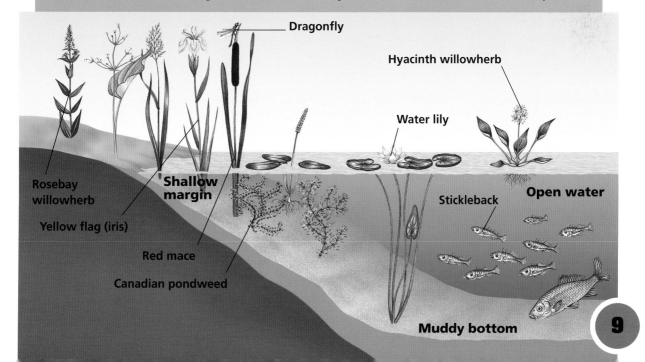

Dragonfly

Hyacinth willowherb

Water lily

Rosebay willowherb

Yellow flag (iris)

Shallow margin

Red mace

Canadian pondweed

Stickleback

Open water

Muddy bottom

What Is the Most Important Land Habitat?

Rain forests are the most important habitats in the world. They cover less than two percent of the earth's surface, but they are home to more than half the world's animals and plants.

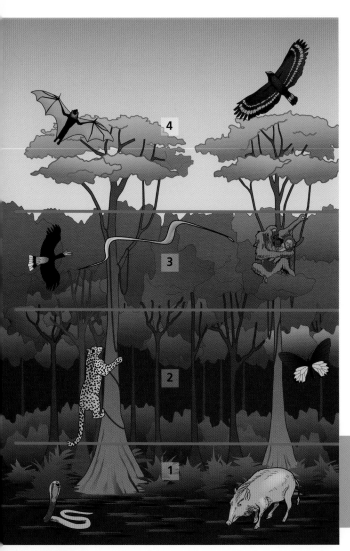

Rain forests are warm and wet all year round. Most are in the **tropics**, but there are also **subtropical** and **temperate** rain forests.

Layered Habitats

A rain forest is not just one habitat—it is several, stacked one on top of the other. Few animals and plants live in the rain forest's lower levels because little sunlight reaches here. Any plants there must be able to survive in deep shade.

The real richness is in the canopy, 100 to 150 feet (30 to 45 meters) up. This is a layer of leafy treetops, with countless other plants growing on the trees' branches. The treetops provide food and shelter for millions of animals, especially insects.

◄ *The layers in the rain forest: the forest floor (1), understory (2), canopy (3) and emergent trees (4).*

Useful Plants

Much of the food we eat originally came from rain forests. Bananas, oranges, cucumbers, cocoa, tea, and sugar cane are a few examples.

Over a quarter of the medicines we use also originate from rain forest plants. Two examples are quinine, used to treat **malaria**, and vincristine, an anticancer drug.

Disappearing Forests

Rain forests are disappearing at an alarming rate. Trees are cut down for timber and to clear land for farms, buildings, and roads. **Conservation** groups and governments are trying to save the rain forests. However, over the last one hundred and fifty years, half the world's rain forests have been destroyed.

◀ *Temperate rain forest on the west coast of the United States.*

RAIN FOREST SOIL

Although rain forests are rich environments, their soil is thin and poor. All the **nutrients** are held in the living plants and animals. Whenever something dies, it rots very quickly. It provides food for insects, or its nutrients are taken in through plants' roots or **fungi**.

What Is the Biggest Land Habitat?

The largest biome on land is another kind of forest, called **boreal forest** or taiga. Taiga is found in regions with short, warm summers and long, cold winters. A wide band of taiga stretches across northern Asia, Europe, and North America.

Needle Leaves

The main trees in boreal forests are firs, pines, and spruces, which are adapted to survive long, harsh winters. Their waxy, needlelike leaves lose little water, which is important in the winter when the water in the ground is frozen. The trees are cone-shaped, which allows them to easily shed snow.

Boreal Wildlife

In summer, insects and birds fly around the forest. Voles, lemmings, and other small rodents provide food for predators such as weasels, foxes, owls, and eagles. The boreal forests also contain larger mammals such as moose, bears, wolves, and lynx.

◄ *Wolves are among the top predators in the taiga. They travel north in the summer to hunt on the tundra.*

Hibernating Trees

South of the boreal forests, where winters are shorter, **deciduous broadleaved** forests grow. There, the trees have thin, broad leaves with a large surface for collecting sunlight and carbon dioxide for **photosynthesis**. They shed their leaves in winter, and become **dormant** in the cold weather.

In the Northern Hemisphere, most natural broadleaved forests have been cut down for farmland.

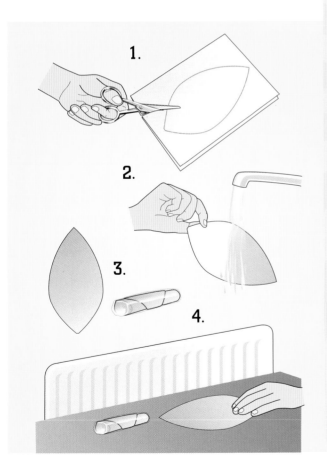

Why Are Grasses Such Successful Plants?

Grasslands cover almost as much land as forests. The largest grasslands are in areas where it is hot in summer and cold in winter, or where it is hot all year with a wet season and a dry season.

Grasslands include the pampas of South America, prairies and plains of North America, steppes of central Asia, and savannas of central and southern Africa.

Well-adapted Plants

Grasslands grow where it is too dry for forests. Grasses store food and water in their roots. The parts of the plant above ground may dry out completely, but once rain falls the plant can regrow from its roots.

Grasses can survive **grazing** because they grow from a point very close to the ground. They can easily regrow after being eaten by buffalo or other wildlife.

Grassland Wildife

Many animals have adapted to eat grasses. Small grass-eaters include caterpillars and rabbits. Large grazers include horses and elephants.

▼ *Lions, the top predators of the African savanna, prey on zebras and other grass-eaters.*

▲ *Gelada baboons are found only in the highlands of Ethiopia. They are grazers, living on grass.*

Owls, eagles, weasels, foxes, and coyotes feed on smaller grass-eaters, while the larger grazers are hunted by lions, leopards, cheetahs, pumas, and wolves.

Because grasslands are so open, large grazing animals are adapted to run to escape their enemies. Predators use stealth to creep up on their prey, or they hunt in packs.

Replaced by Farms

The wild grassland in many parts of the world has been replaced either by fields of grain, or **cereals**, or by grazing areas for domestic sheep and cattle. Many wild grassland species are endangered because their habitat has disappeared.

SCIENCE SECRETS

WASTE REMOVAL

Dung beetles feed on manure, usually that of grazing animals such as deer and zebras. Some kinds simply live and feed in piles of dung. Others roll the manure into a ball, and bury it. Feeding on dung sounds disgusting, but in fact these animals are an important part of the habitat. Without them it would take much longer for waste to rot into the soil.

What Are the Most Extreme Habitats?

A poor habitat is one that cannot support many living things. Hot deserts and tundra (cold deserts) are both very poor biomes.

No Rain

A desert is an area that has very little rainfall—less than 10 inches (25 centimeters) per year. Some deserts are extremely dry. Parts of the Atacama Desert in South America have not had any rainfall for four hundred years!

Desert Survival

Desert plants survive in one of two ways. Some have a thick, waxy coating to keep in water. They also store water in swollen stems or leaves. Other plants survive by growing, flowering, and producing seeds very quickly whenever it rains.

Most desert animals are small. Many rest underground by day and feed in the cool of the night.

◀ A sidewinder snake. Reptiles, scorpions, and spiders are common desert animals.

Arctic Cold

Tundra is a cold, empty habitat close to the Arctic. As in hot deserts, there is little rainfall. The ground is permanently frozen (permafrost). In summer, the top part of the soil becomes wet and spongy.

Plants able to survive the tundra's freezing winds include low-growing grasses, mosses, and shrubs.

DESERT AND TUNDRA

Try creating desert conditions for plants and see how they grow.

You will need:
• two plastic pots • some soil or potting compost • some sand • grass seeds

1. Put some soil in one pot, and some sand in the other. Push in a few grass seeds.

2. Add a little water to the pot with soil but not the one with sand. Put both pots on a sunny windowsill.

3. Check the pots once a day. Each time, add a little water to the pot with soil. What happens?

Most plants do not grow well in dry conditions. The grass in the "desert" pot may not grow at all.

◀ *Tundra animals include caribou (reindeer). When snow covers the ground, caribou scrape it aside and feed on the mosses beneath.*

What Makes Mountain Habitats Different?

Mountains can be found in any biome. A mountain range might rise out of an area of grassland, or it might be surrounded by forest. However, the mountain is a habitat all of its own, different from the surrounding area.

Changing With Height

Like rain forests, mountains contain different habitats at different heights.

Mountain tops are harsh environments that may be cold, windy, and often snow-covered. Few plants can survive, and much of the ground is bare rock. Mosses and **lichens** grow on some of the rocks, though, and some insects and spiders live there.

Some mountain ranges, such as the Alps in Europe and the Himalayas in Asia, have pastures that burst briefly

▼ *Andean condors are the world's largest birds of prey. They live in the Andes Mountains in South America.*

▲ *Steady on their feet, llamas live in the Andes Mountains. Their thick, shaggy coats keep them warm.*

into flower in spring. Lower down on mountains is the **treeline**, below which trees grow. The conifers at higher altitudes give way to broadleaved trees or rain forest on the lower slopes.

Mountain Animals

Animals specialized for high mountain living must survive bitter cold, strong winds, and steep, rocky ground. Snow leopards, mountain goats, and mountain gorillas have thick, warm coats and are very agile.

HIGH JUMPER

High in the Himalayas lives a small spider that could be the highest permanent resident in the world. The Himalayan jumping spider is a well-equipped predator. It has keen eyesight and can jump nearly thirty times its body length.

At lower levels, the spider stalks springtails and other small insects. At around 22,000 feet (6,700 m), its only food is insects blown by the wind from lower levels.

Why Are Island Habitats So Special?

Island habitats vary from sandy tropical paradises to outcrops of rocks pounded by cold seas. Islands do share one thing in common, however. Their inhabitants are generally under more threat than mainland animals and plants.

Unique Species

Most island species are cut off from others like them. Over many years, they adapt to conditions on the island. Island foxes, for example, are found only on

▼ *Many islands are formed when a volcano erupts out of the sea. Mount Rishiri, on Rishiri Island in Japan, is an inactive volcano.*

► Coquerel's sifaka is a type of lemur. Like most other lemurs it is endangered—it is found in only two protected areas on Madagascar.

islands off the coast of California. They are smaller than other foxes because they have adapted to the smaller prey on the islands.

New Zealand has many ground-nesting birds found nowhere else. This is because, until humans arrived, the only native mammals were two kinds of bat. The birds had few predators and were able to nest safely down on the ground.

Fragile Habitats

Island habitats are easily damaged because many are small and are home to highly specialized species. Humans are often the cause of the destruction. In Madagascar, huge areas of forest have been cut down, endangering lemurs, chameleons, and other unusual forest animals.

Another danger on an island is the introduction of foreign species. In New Zealand, rats, cats, and other predators brought by humans killed off many of the native birds.

ISLAND SECRETS

The scientist Charles Darwin visited the Galapagos Islands in 1835. He observed and collected many animals and plants there that helped him develop his **theory of evolution**.

Darwin noticed that there were many species of finches, some found on only one tiny island. He suggested that originally there had been a single finch species. Over time, this species had evolved into many others, as the birds adapted to different diets and ways of life.

What Are Local Habitats?

Biomes are particular kinds of habitat that are found across the world. Each biome has many different habitats within it.

Variable Biomes

The forest biome, for example, includes the oak forests of northern Europe and the beech and maple forests in eastern North America. Different species make their homes in these different forest habitats.

Lions and giraffes live on the savanna grasslands of southern Africa, while coyotes and bison are found on the American prairies.

▼ *In spring, woodland trees begin to grow new leaves and bluebells take advantage of the light to flower.*

▲ *A female dragonfly lays her eggs in a forest pond.*

Local Variants

Even within a particular region, a biome has many habitats. One area of a deciduous forest may have mainly beech trees, while another section has oaks. In areas with poor soil or low rainfall, the forest may have few trees and just scrubby bushes and grasses.

All these different habitats can be found in one region with a similar climate.

DISCOVER LOCAL HABITATS

Can you find different habitats? Explore the area near where you live. Go with an adult or ask permission to look around with a group of friends.

You will need:
- a notebook
- pencils
- camera (optional)

1. Choose two different areas—for example, a woodland area and a river, or a seashore and swamp.

2. Go to each habitat, and spend 30 minutes or so there. What plants grow there? Sit quietly, looking and listening. What wildlife do you see or hear? Look among plants and under stones for insect life. Remember to put stones back where they were.

3. Write down what you find. Take photographs if possible, as this will make it easier to identify species that you don't know.

What are the differences in the plants and animals living in the two local habitats?

How Small Can a Habitat Be?

Within a large biome there are many different habitats—and within each of those habitats are even smaller habitats.

So how small can a habitat get? For a small animal or plant, it can be very small indeed!

Habitats On a Tree

There are many different habitats on a single tree. Beetles, worms, and other creatures live around the roots and in the **leaf litter**. Mosses and lichens grow on the bark, and insects live in cracks within it. Some beetle **larvae** bore tunnels into the wood itself.

In the canopy, insects and other small animals feed on leaves, sap, flowers, and fruit. Insect predators such as ladybugs and wasps feed on these plant-eaters. This entire living community can be different on each kind of tree.

▼ *The tracks of a leaf miner in a leaf. Leaf miners are the larvae of insects (mostly moths) that live and feed inside leaves.*

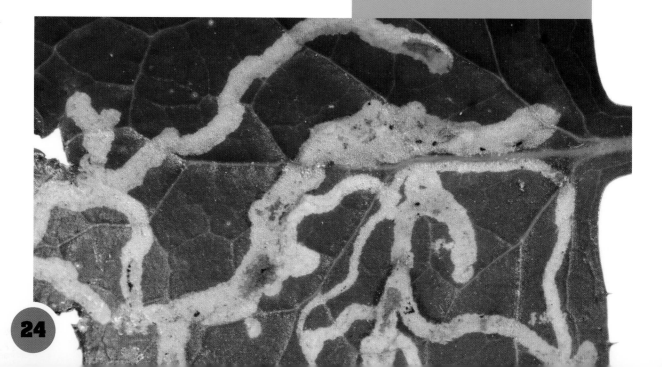

▲ *Tiny varroa mites attach to bees and feed on their blood. The mites can kill off whole bee colonies, because when they feed they pass on disease.*

Going Even Smaller

Some microhabitats are even smaller than different parts of a tree. Mites and fleas are **parasites** that live on other animals. Varroa mites are small enough to live on insects, while demodex mites live on human eyebrows!

For **bacteria** and other microbes, just about any area can be a habitat. Some fungi and bacteria live inside plant roots. Some cause damage, but others help plants get nutrients from the soil, and in return feed on sugars from the plants.

Most animals have bacteria living on their skin, their teeth, and in their gut, where they help to **digest** food.

SCIENCE SECRETS

UNDER THE MICROSCOPE

Scientists at the Massachusetts Institute of Technology (MIT) have been experimenting with microhabitats the size of a microscope slide. They use these habitats to study how microscopic sea creatures find food in the oceans.

How Do Humans Affect Habitats?

Humans have completely changed many natural habitats. They have cut down forests, cleared grasslands, and drained **wetlands** to make way for cities, towns, farmland, and **plantations**.

Many species have become **extinct** or endangered because of habitat destruction. However, some animals and plants have adapted to survive.

Springing Up Everywhere

The plants that survive best in human-made habitats are those that spread widely, grow quickly, and can cope with poor soil or in shady places. Examples are dock, couch grass, and yarrow. They are all plants that gardeners and farmers call weeds.

◀ An urban fox goes through rubbish looking for food. Foxes are most active at night, but they also scavenge by day.

▲ *In North America, bears visit the edges of cities and towns to find easy pickings in rubbish dumps.*

Adaptable Animals

Animals that survive in towns, cities, and other human habitats are very adaptable. They are often omnivores (they eat both plants and animals), and **scavengers**, feeding on dead or rotting animals and other waste food.

Some of the most successful animals are pests such as cockroaches and rats. Other species that have adapted to life around humans include house spiders, geckos, opossums, raccoons, foxes, and many species of birds.

SCIENCE SECRETS

CITY FALCONS

During the 1950s and 1960s, the numbers of peregrine falcons in Europe and North America dropped. A **pesticide** called DDT was poisoning the birds and damaging their eggs.

In the 1970s, many countries banned the use of DDT. Peregrine falcon numbers slowly recovered. The birds began to nest in cities. In the wild, peregrines are often found on cliffs. In cities, the birds nest on artificial cliffs—skyscrapers.

How Can We Save Disappearing Habitats?

Today, the earth is facing the mass extinction of thousands of species. Most of this is due to human activity—the biggest cause is habitat destruction. How can we save our disappearing habitats?

Preserving Habitats

Important habitats can be preserved as national parks or conservation areas. In these areas, laws protect the habitat and wildlife. However, even in national parks there can be **poaching**.

Sometimes natural habitats can only be preserved in small areas. Big predators

▼ *Tourism provides a way for local people to earn money from a habitat without destroying it.*

such as tigers and wolves cannot find enough food in these pockets of land. One solution is wildlife corridors, or strips of protected land that allow animals to move from one area to another. Rivers, canals, and disused roads or railways can make good corridors.

Rescuing Habitats

It is possible to rescue some lost habitats and save the living things that rely on them. Some wetlands have been rescued by restoring the natural drainage and replanting reeds and other plants.

Preserving and restoring habitats takes time and effort, but it is vital for the health of the whole world.

ENCOURAGING WILDLIFE

There are many different ways to encourage wildlife to come to your home.

You will need:
- a garden or window box
- seeds or small plants • bird food • bird or bat boxes (optional)

1. Plant flowers in your garden or window box that blossom at different times to encourage bees and insects. In turn, these will attract birds and other insect-eaters. Find plants that will provide seeds and fruit to feed birds and other animals in autumn, too.

2. Put out water and food for the birds—especially in cold, winter months.

3. If you have a garden, provide bird and bat boxes. Ask your parents if you can leave a pile of rotting logs or branches as a home for beetles and other insects.

4. Let a small area of garden become overgrown. This will provide a place where animals can rest and shelter.

Glossary

bacterium (plural bacteria) A very tiny, simple living thing that has just a single cell.

biome A particular type of habitat found across the world, for example water or grassland.

boreal forest Also known as taiga. A type of conifer forest found in cold climates. A band of boreal forest stretches across northern Asia, Europe, and North America.

breed To produce offspring (young).

broadleaved Describes a tree or shrub with broad, flat leaves, not narrow leaves (like grasses) or needlelike leaves (like conifers). Many broadleaved trees are deciduous.

cereal A food crop that is a type of grass. Examples include rice, wheat, maize, and barley.

conifer A tree with dark green, needlelike leaves that produces its seeds inside cones. Pines, firs, spruces, redwoods, and yews are all conifers.

conservation The work of scientists and other concerned people to preserve disappearing habitats and living things, and to reduce the effects of pollution on the natural environment.

deciduous Describes a plant that loses its leaves in winter or during the dry season.

digest To break down food so that it can be used by a living thing.

dormant Deeply asleep or in a resting state.

evaporation When a liquid turns into a gas. If you leave water outside, the Sun's heat makes some of it escape into the air as water vapor.

extinct Describes a species that has died out.

fungus (plural fungi) A plantlike living thing that often gets its food from dead plants or animal material. Mushrooms and molds are both types of fungus.

grazing Eating grass (as the main part of a diet).

larva (plural larvae) The young stage of an animal, usually an insect. The larva looks very different from the adult.

leaf litter The fallen leaves that carpet the floor of some types of forest for all or part of the year.

lichen A plantlike living thing that is actually a partnership between algae and fungi. Lichen forms crusty patches or bushy growths on trees, rocks, old walls, and other surfaces.

malaria A dangerous tropical disease, which is passed through bites from infected mosquitoes.

nutrient A simple chemical found in food, which provides nourishment so that an organism can live and grow.

offspring The young of an animal.

organism A living thing such as an animal or plant.

parasite A living thing that survives in or on another living thing, taking nutrients from it.

pesticide A chemical used in farming to kill off insects or other pests that eat crops.

photosynthesis A process that plants use to turn light energy from the Sun into plant matter.

phytoplankton Microscopic plants that float in the waters of the ocean.

plantation A specialized kind of farm, often found in tropical areas, where large areas are used to grow crops such as tea or palm trees.

poaching Illegal killing of protected animals.

pollen The powdery substance produced by a flower that contains male sex cells. When pollen comes into contact with female sex cells (ovules), the plant can produce a seed.

predator An animal that hunts and eats other animals for food.

prey An animal (usually a plant-eater) that is hunted by predators.

reproduce To create offspring.

sap The sugary liquid inside plants that is carried along tubes (called phloem) from the leaves to feed other parts of the plant.

scavenger An animal that eats the remains of dead animals and any other waste material.

sewage Waste water from houses and factories.

species One particular type of animal or plant. Members of the same species look similar and can breed together in the wild.

subtropical Relating to the area between the tropical and temperate regions, where the climate is often warm or hot and can be very dry.

temperate Relating to the two regions of the earth that lie between the equator and the North Pole and South Pole, where the climate is warm in summer and cold in winter.

territory The area that an animal defends against other animals, usually of the same species.

theory of evolution The scientific explanation of how living things gradually change, or evolve, over long periods to adapt to their surroundings.

treeline The level on a mountain above which no trees grow.

tropics The hot, mainly wet region immediately north and south of the equator.

ultraviolet light Radiation similar to light that humans cannot see but some animals can.

wetland Marshland, swamp, or other kinds of wet, boggy habitat.

zooplankton Very small or miroscopic sea animals that drift with the ocean currents.

Further Information

Books
Grasslands Under Threat by Paul Mason (Heinemann-Raintree, 2009)

Last Chance To See by Douglas Adams and Mark Carwardine (Arrow, 2009)

Science, The Facts: Habitats by Rebecca Hunter (Franklin Watts, 2007)

The Taiga: Life in the Boreal Forest by Laurie Peach Toupin (Franklin Watts, 2005)

The Vanishing Rainforest by Richard Platt and Rupert van Wyck (Frances Lincoln, 2004)

Websites
BBC Science and Nature: Sea Life
(www.bbc.co.uk/nature/blueplanet/)
Information about ocean life.

Blue Planet Biomes: World Biomes
(www.blueplanetbiomes.org/world_biomes.htm)
An overview of many different biomes.

Earth Observatory: Mission Biomes
(www.earthobservatory.nasa.gov/Experiments/Biome)
Information and activities related to biomes.

Habitats: Home Sweet Home
(www.nationalgeographic.com/geography-action/habitats.html)
Features on habitats from National Geographic.

RSPB (Royal Society for the Protection of Birds)
(www.rspb.org.uk)
An organization dedicated to protecting birds, with advice on how to make your garden a better habitat for birds and other wildlife.

World National Parks
(www.world-national-parks.net)
Information on national parks in your country and around the world.

Index